TEN LITTLE SISTERS

Illustrated by Lana Hill

Text by Virginia Rackley, Deloris Hart, Rhita Brniak, Mary Hickmott, Irma Swierk Allen, Pauline Ariel, Phyllis Ferguson, Vera Barber, Audrey Alford, & Doris Wenzel

Based on the non-fiction book, *Ten Sisters: A True Story*, by the same authors

Mayhaven Publishing

P O Box 557
Mahomet, IL 61853 USA

ISBN 1-878044-38-9
Printed in Canada

Jenny

DoDo

Bede

Phyllis

Vera

Margy

Irma

Bertie

Audrey

Doris

We lived in Paradise Township with our parents and our brothers, Carl and Jessie Dale, in a teeny-tiny house.

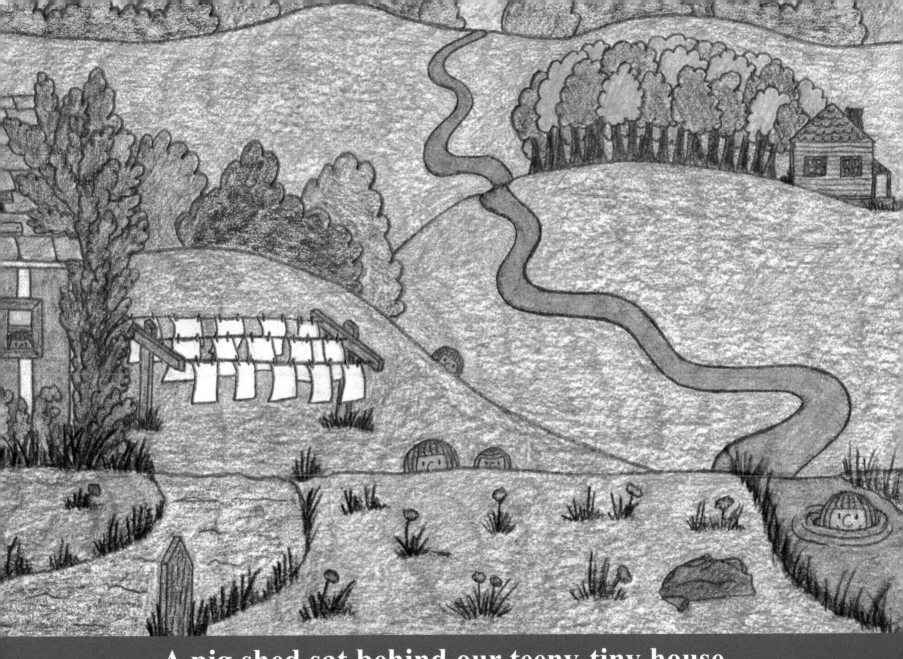

**A pig shed sat behind our teeny-tiny house,
and behind the pig shed was a hill leading to Grandma's house.**

We sisters all slept together.

We had lots of things to do.

Sometimes we jumped on the bed.

We dressed up fence posts and named them
Mrs. Liggeley and Mrs. Jumeley.

We rolled down the hill.

We pestered the goat.

We played "house" in the pig shed.
Carl threw stones against the shed and made Jenny cry.

We played in the creek.

Sometimes we hid beneath the bridge.

We made movies
with an old sheet and a flashlight.

We waited for Dodo to fix our hair.

Irma's favorite thing was climbing trees.

We liked to sing.
You Are My Sunshine was a favorite song.

We built a boxing ring.

Our friends liked to box, too.

Dad hunted rabbits and squirrels to eat.

We helped him fish.

Bertie was the smartest student.

Phyllis loved going to Zion Hill Church.

Bede hurt her leg climbing Grandma's peach tree.

Margy was very sick when we had the measles.
Mom had to take care of all of us.

One day Carl and Jessie Dale left home.

We missed them.

Later, we were taken to a courthouse in a neighboring town.

We didn't know we wouldn't return to the teeny-tiny house.

When we got to the courthouse
someone took our picture.
Someone else asked us to sing,
but we didn't feel like singing.

At the end of that day, each of us went, alone,
to a new place to live.
Doris and Audrey were given new names.
Vera went home with Grandma and Grandpa Coen.

It would be a long, long time until we were all together again.

We were very sad.
We thought of one another.

Then, Jenny, Dodo and Bede found each other.
Eventually, they found the rest of us.

Now we meet once a year at a big reunion
with our children, and grandchildren,
and great grandchildren.

One great big family.

Getting to know one another again makes us happy.